I Feel Sad

Kelly Doudna

Published by SandCastle™, an imprint of ABDO Publishing Company, 4940 Viking Drive, Edina, Minnesota 55435.

Printed in the United States.

Photo credits: Corel, Digital Stock, Digital Vision, PhotoDisc

Library of Congress Cataloging-in-Publication Data

Doudna, Kelly, 1963-
    I feel sad / Kelly Doudna.
       p. cm. -- (How do you feel?)
    Summary: In photographs and simple text, children contrast things that make them feel sad with those that do not, knowing that the sadness will pass.
    ISBN 1-57765-189-8
    1. Sadness in children--Juvenile literature. [1. Sadness.]
  I. Title. II. Series: Doudna, Kelly, 1963- How do you feel?
    BF723.S15D68 1998
    152.4--dc21

                                                         98-26676
                                                              CIP
                                                               AC

The SandCastle concept, content, and reading method have been reviewed and approved by a national advisory board including literacy specialists, librarians, elementary school teachers, early childhood education professionals, and parents.

Let Us Know

After reading the book, SandCastle would like you to tell us your stories about reading. What is your favorite page? Was there something hard that you needed help with? Share the ups and downs of learning to read. We want to hear from you! To get posted on the Abdo Publishing Company Web site, send us email at:

sandcastle@abdopub.com

About SandCastle™
Nonfiction books for the beginning reader

- Basic concepts of phonics are incorporated with integrated language methods of reading instruction. Most words are short, and phrases, letter sounds, and word sounds are repeated.

- Readability is determined by the number of words in each sentence, the number of characters in each word, and word lists based on curriculum frameworks.

- Full-color photography reinforces word meanings and concepts.

- "Words I Can Read" list at the end of each book teaches basic elements of grammar, helps the reader recognize the words in the text, and builds vocabulary.

- Reading levels are indicated by the number of flags on the castle.

Look for more SandCastle books in these three reading levels:

Level 1
(one flag)

Level 2
(two flags)

Level 3
(three flags)

Grades Pre-K to K
5 or fewer words per page

Grades K to 1
5 to 10 words per page

Grades 1 to 2
10 to 15 words per page

I feel sad when no one
wants to play with me.

I am not sad when my
sister and I play dress up.

I feel sad when no one
wants to be with me.

I am not sad when I laugh
with Mom and Dad.

I feel sad when my friends will not let me play in their game.

I am not sad when Mom
and I kick a ball in the park.

I feel sad when I think about Grandpa and visit his grave.

I am not sad when I bring flowers to Grandma and cheer her up.

It is okay for me to feel sad.

Later, I will not feel sad.

Words I Can Read

Nouns

A noun is a person, place, or thing

ball (BAWL) p. 15
Dad (DAD) p. 11
dress up
   (DRESS uhp) p. 7
game (GAME) p. 13
Grandma
   (GRAND-mah) p. 19

Grandpa
   (GRAND-pah) p. 17
grave (GRAYV) p. 17
Mom (MOM) pp. 11, 15
park (PARK) p. 15
sister (SISS-tur) p. 7

Plural Nouns

A plural noun is more than one
person, place, or thing

flowers
   (FLOW-urz) p. 19

friends (FRENDZ) p. 13

Pronouns

A pronoun is a word that replaces a noun

her (HUR) p. 19
I (EYE) pp. 5, 7, 9, 11, 13, 15,
   17, 19, 21
it (IT) p. 21

me (MEE) pp. 5, 9, 13, 21
no one
   (NOH wuhn) pp. 5, 9

22

Verbs

A verb is an action or being word

am (AM) pp. 7, 11, 15, 19
be (BEE) p. 9
bring (BRING) p. 19
cheer (CHIHR) p. 19
feel (FEEL) pp. 5, 9, 13, 17, 21
is (IZ) p. 21
kick (KIK) p. 15

laugh (LAF) p. 11
let (LET) p. 13
play (PLAY) pp. 5, 7, 13
think (THINGK) p. 17
visit (VIZ-it) p. 17
wants (WONTSS) pp. 5, 9
will (WIL) pp. 13, 21

Adjectives

An adjective describes something

his (HIZ) p. 17
my (MYE) pp. 7, 13
okay (oh-KAY) p. 21

sad (SAD) pp. 5, 7, 9, 11, 13, 15, 17, 19, 21
their (THAIR) p. 13

Adverbs

An adverb tells how, when, or where something happens

later (LATE-ur) p. 21

up (UHP) p. 19

Glossary

friends - People you like being with and know well.

grave - A place where a dead person is buried.

park - Land set apart for people or animals.